Sam Stays Safe

WRITTEN BY CLARE MISHICA
ILLUSTRATED BY JILL DUBIN

Cover design: Robert Glover.

ISBN 0-7847-1923-3

12 11 10 09 08 07 06 9 8 7 6 5 4 3 2 1

Cincinnati, Ohio

“This is a big store,” Mama said.

“Stay close.”

“We will,” said Samantha.

She whirled and twirled around with Bear.

Mama looked at dresses.

She picked up a bright red dress

with a purple scarf.

Samantha whirled and twirled some more.

"Oh, no," said Samantha
as she stopped spinning.
"I think I left Bear in the garden
department!"

Samantha looked over her shoulder.

Mama told me to stay close,

but I'll only be gone a minute, she thought.

Samantha hurried back

to the garden department.

Bear was where she had left him!

Samantha skipped back to the dresses.

“Here we are!” she giggled.

But Mama wasn’t there.

“Mama?” Samantha called.

Samantha ran down one aisle

and up another.

She still did not see her mother.

Samantha’s stomach felt
like a roller coaster.
Hot tears slipped down Samantha’s cheeks.
“Dear God,” Samantha prayed.
“I’m scared and I can’t find my Mama.”

Then Samantha remembered a song.

If you're lost in a store, what do you do?

Ask a friendly store clerk—she'll help you.

March to the cash register—one, two, three.

Don't be afraid.

Clerks can find your family.

“God helped me remember Mama’s song.
I know what to do!” Samantha told Bear.
“I’ll be brave and ask for help.”
Samantha wiped her tears
and walked up to the front of the store.

"Hello," said Samantha to the clerk.
"Can you help me and Bear
find my mother?"

The clerk smiled and took her hand.
"Sure I can," she said.
"We will make an announcement
that everyone in the store will hear.
What's your name?"
"Samantha Baker,"
said Samantha.

Soon a happy voice said, “Samantha!”

It was Mama’s voice.

Samantha gave her mother a giant hug.

“I’m so glad I found you,” said Mama.

"Why didn't you stay with me?"

"I'm sorry," said Samantha.

"Bear and I are going to stay very close now."

"That's good," said Mama.

Then she gave Samantha and Bear another hug. Samantha smiled the happiest and biggest smile of all.